cks Are Birds

(But, Not All Birds Are Ducks)

Written & Illustrated by

Tara Michele Zrinski

AuthorHouse™
1663 Liberty Drive
Bloomington, IN 47403
www.authorhouse.com
Phone: 1 (800) 839-8640

Published by AuthorHouse 11/21/2015

ISBN: 978-1-5049-6008-3 (sc)
978-1-5049-6010-6 (hc)
978-1-5049-6009-0 (e)

Library of Congress Control Number: 2015918571

Print information available on the last page.

Any people depicted in stock imagery provided by Thinkstock are models,
and such images are being used for illustrative purposes only.
Certain stock imagery © Thinkstock.

Cover art, "Yellow Duck and Ducklings," inspired with permission from photographer Gary Kramer. "Swimming Ostrich"
inspired with permission by photography taken by Vandit Kalia @ photosafariindia.com.

This book is printed on acid-free paper.

authorHOUSE®

All Ducks Are Birds
(but, not all birds are ducks)

Written and Illustrated by

Tara Michele Zrinski

This book is dedicated to my son, Bryton,
who inspires me everyday
to ask questions and find answers.

Special thanks to all the friends and family
who financially supported this endeavor and, especially,
Scott, whose tech savvy brought out the best in my art.

NOTE TO PARENTS:

This story is based on a conversation I had with my son over a decade ago when he was four years old. On one of many walks to Monocacy Creek to visit the ducks, he asked, "Mommy, are all birds ducks?" At first, I thought it was such a silly question but, I found myself automatically responding, "Not all birds are ducks." I realized we were *doing* logic.

Aristotelian logic is the cornerstone of Western thought. We use logic to categorize and understand our observations of reality. Children are naturally trying to understand the world around them and crave ways to communicate what they observe.

This book uses syllogisms to explore the relationships of different types of birds and their characteristics to each other by introducing children to simple patterns of logic. Children learn that just because certain statements about some birds are true, that they do not necessarily mean they are true for all birds. "Some birds fly," Other birds seem the same but, are not. "Penguins and puffins are black and white but, puffins are not penguins."

Between the ages of 3 and 6, children are gaining cognitive skills based on their natural inclination to explore the world and question their surroundings. They are moving from concrete, black and white thinking where *all* birds are ducks to understanding that ducks are only a small category of birds.

Children are also learning the language skills to communicate that *some* and *not all* are statements used to qualify their observations. Their ability to communicate their observations leads to intellectual mastery of higher orders of thinking from which they will benefit over the course of their lives.

Parents can use this book to start a conversation with their children, much like the one I had with my son, which will help children to become more fully aware and engaged with the reality they observe, while inspiring a deep and meaningful inquiry of the world.

All ducks are birds,
but, not *all* birds are ducks.

All geese are birds,
but, *no* geese are ducks.

All swans are birds,
but, *no* swans are ducks.

Just because geese and swans are birds,
and ducks are birds, doesn't mean that
geese and swans are ducks.
Not *all* birds are ducks.

All geese can fly.

All swans can fly.

All ducks can fly.

If all geese, swans and ducks can fly, then all birds can fly, right?

No! Not *all* birds can fly.

All ostriches are birds,
but, ostriches cannot fly.

Not *all* birds can fly, but,
all birds have feathers.

Even penguins.

All penguins have feathers,
but, penguins cannot fly.

What about puffins?

Puffins can fly.

Are puffins flying penguins?

Penguins are black and white.

Puffins are black and white.

Puffins are *not* penguins.

Just because both penguins and puffins are black and white does not mean they are *all* penguins.

Puffins are birds. Penguins are birds, but, penguins are not puffins.

All penguins are birds, but,
not *all* birds are penguins.

All penguins swim, except
baby penguins.

They are not ready yet.

All geese swim.

All swans swim.

All ducks swim.

If penguins, geese, swans and ducks swim, and *all* penguins, geese, swans, and ducks are birds, then, all birds *must* swim, right?

No! Ostriches do *not* swim.

Some ostriches sit in puddles.

Sitting in puddles is *not* swimming.

So, not *all* birds swim.

All birds lay eggs, though.

Even ostriches.

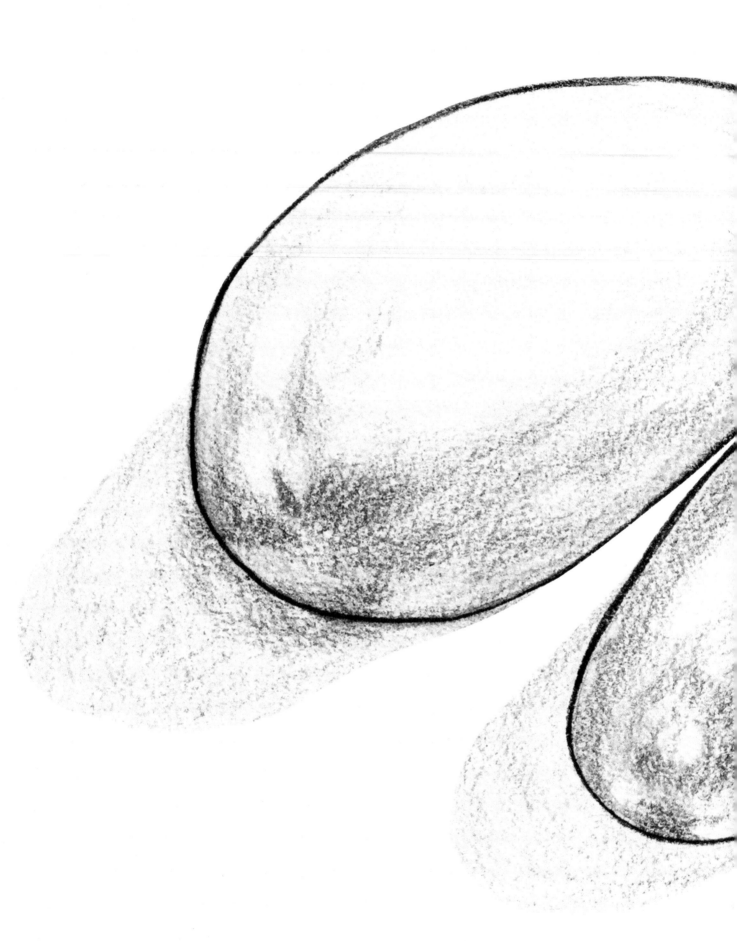

Geese lay eggs.

Swans lay eggs.

Ducks lay eggs.

Guess which egg is a duck's egg.

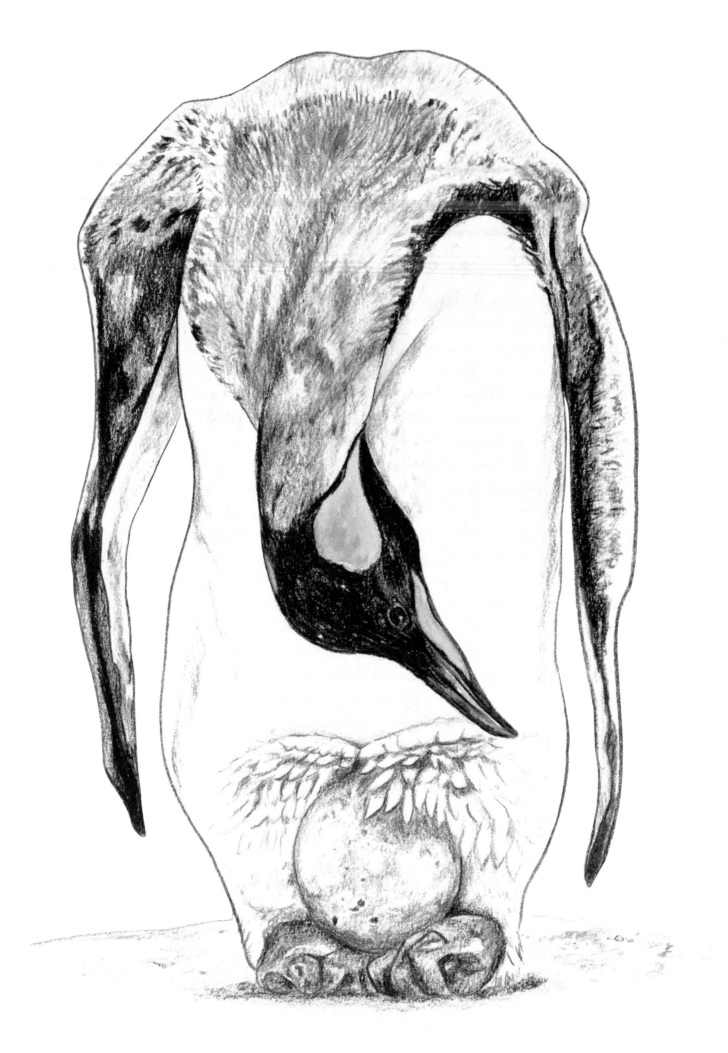

Even penguins lay eggs.

All birds lay eggs, but, not *all* birds are penguins.

Some birds are ostriches.

Some birds are geese.

Some birds are swans.

Some birds are ducks.

Not *all* birds are ducks.

All birds have feathers.

All birds lay eggs.

Some birds fly.

Some birds swim.

Some birds fly and swim.

But, not *all* birds are the same.

Even though not all birds are the same,
all birds are beautiful and unique.

Just like you.

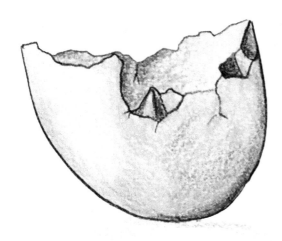

THE END

About the Author

 Tara is an Adjunct Professor of Philosophy at Northampton Community College. She has also been a freelance writer since 2009, her career is highlighted by a weekly parenting column on BethlehemPatch.com, monthly blogs on Shalereporter.com and bi-annual feature articles in the Elucidator Magazine as well as several academic articles.

Since she was a child, nature has inspired her artistic endeavors. She has shown and sold her acrylic paintings in cafes, restaurants and galleries. All of her birds are drawn in colored pencils, creating a level of control, detail and color that make the birds jump off the page.

Tara lives with her family and their two cats in Bethlehem, Pennsylvania. She studied Philosophy and English at Drew University and holds Master's Degrees from Moravian Theological Seminary in Theological Studies and Pastoral Counseling. She loves to share stories, trips to the bookstore and longs walks to visit the ducks. Tara is active in her community as an environmental activist, volunteering as a Local Coordinator for Food and Water Watch.

CPSIA information can be obtained
at www.ICGtesting.com
Printed in the USA
LVOW06*2328130617
538032LV00008B/23/P